Contents

		page
Introduction		v
Historical Notes		vi
Chapter 1	Moscow, 1901	1
Chapter 2	Summer, 1903	2
Chapter 3	1905	3
Chapter 4	January, 1906	6
Chapter 5	Christmas, 1911	10
Chapter 6	1915, During World War I	16
Chapter 7	Winter, 1916	19
Chapter 8	1917	20
Chapter 9	1918	34
Chapter 10	1919	42
Chapter 11	1919–21	45
Chapter 12	Spring, 1922	63
Chapter 13	Summer, 1929	64
Chapter 14	Summer, 1943	67
Activities		69

Doctor Zhivago

BORIS PASTERNAK

Level 5

Retold by Nancy Stanley
Series Editors: Andy Hopkins and Jocelyn Potter

Pearson Education Limited
Edinburgh Gate, Harlow,
Essex CM20 2JE, England
and Associated Companies throughout the world.

ISBN 0 582 41695 7

First published in Great Britain by Collins and Harvill 1958
© Giangiacomo Feltrinelli Editore 1958
© in the English translation Harvill 1958
This adaptation first published by Penguin Books 1998
Published by Addison Wesley Longman Limited and Penguin Books Ltd. 1998
New edition first published 1999

Third impression 2001

Text copyright © Nancy Stanley 1998
Illustrations copyright © MGM courtesy of The Ronald Grant Archive
All rights reserved

The moral right of the adapter and of the photographer has been asserted

Typeset by Digital Type, London
Set in 11/14pt Bembo
Printed in Spain by Mateu Cromo, S.A. Pinto (Madrid)

Published by Pearson Education Limited in association with
Penguin Books Ltd., both companies being subsidiaries of Pearson Plc

For a complete list of the titles available in the Penguin Readers series please write to your local
Pearson Education office or to: Marketing Department, Penguin Longman Publishing,
5 Bentinck Street, London W1M 5RN.

Introduction

*'Street fighting in Petersburg! The soldiers have joined the rebels! It's the
Revolution!'*

It is the beginning of the twentieth century and the lives of four
young people are interrupted by the extraordinary events of the
Russian Revolution. They struggle to define their roles in a
constantly changing world, just as their country searches for its
way forward. Each of the four – Yury, Tonya, Lara and Pasha –
finds love and loses it, faces the endless problems caused by the
Revolution, and comes to a better understanding of who they
are. They are surrounded by a crowd of unusual, often tragic
figures whose personal histories mirror this formative period in
Russia's history.

Boris Pasternak was born in Moscow in 1890. His father was a
painter and his mother a concert pianist and he grew up in a
world of music and literature. He originally studied music but
gave it up to write poems when he was eighteen. His third book
of poems, *My Sister, Life,* made him famous. Pasternak wrote
stories as well as poems during the 1920s and 1930s. He was not
accepted as an official 'Soviet writer', however, and none of his
works was printed between 1933 and 1943. During that time he
made his living as a translator. *Dr Zhivago* is Pasternak's greatest
work. The government did not allow it to be printed in the
USSR but it appeared in Italy in 1957 and won the Nobel Prize
for Literature in 1958. Because of his problems with the Soviet
government, Pasternak did not accept the prize. Pasternak lived
most of his life in Moscow and died in 1960.

Historical Notes

Doctor Zhivago covers an extremely important time in Russian history. The first parts of the story take place in 1901 and 1903, and then the action moves to 1905. This was the year of the first Russian Revolution, which was a battle between the government of Nicholas II, the last tsar of Russia (tsar is the Russian word for king), and groups of industrial workers, peasants and soldiers. These groups wanted a system of government that would be fair to everyone, especially to the country's poor. Unfortunately, the government did not keep its promises to give basic rights to all Russians, and a growing number of people continued to demand change.

Between 1914 and 1918, many Russians were fighting in World War I, but this did not stop the revolutionary movement. There were two parts to the revolution in 1917. The first happened in February: the government of Tsar Nicholas II was ended (he and his family were murdered in July, 1917), and a new Provisional Government, with a parliament, was put in its place.

The second part of the 1917 revolution happened that October. There were fewer battles and the Bolsheviks, led by Lenin, took over the government and formed a Soviet of People's Commissars. The Bolsheviks were the part of the Social Democratic Party in Russia that believed in revolutionary methods and Marxist principles. They put in place the Dictatorship of the Proletariat.

The new government still had to face many problems. The Russian Civil War (1918–21) was fought between the White Army, who were against Marxism and the new government, and the Bolsheviks or Red Army. After many long and fierce battles, the Red Army finally won and the Union of Soviet Socialist Republics was set up.

Chapter 1   Moscow, 1901

The small, sad group walked behind the horse and carriage which carried the coffin of Marya Nikolayevna. As they walked, they sang 'Eternal Memory'. People along the way stared and made the sign of the cross. Some asked who was in the coffin. 'Zhivago,' they were told, 'but not the great man himself, it's his wife.' The coffin was closed and put into the ground. Earth was thrown on top of it, and suddenly, a ten-year-old boy threw himself on top of the earth. Like a wild animal which has lost its mother, the small boy covered his face with his hands and burst into tears. Finally, his uncle, the dead woman's brother, led him away.

The boy, Yury Andreyevich Zhivago, was now an orphan, even though his father was still alive. He had left Yury and his mother a long time ago and had gone to Siberia. Since then he had spent the family's millions on bad business plans, women and alcohol. Yury didn't know his father, but he could remember something about his own past. Many things used to carry his name. There were Zhivago factories, a Zhivago bank, Zhivago buildings, even a Zhivago cake. When he was younger, Yury had lived in a wonderful house in a beautiful park. He had enjoyed the best of everything. Then one day it all disappeared, and he and his mother became poor.

Now his mother was dead and he was leaving Moscow with her brother, Nikolay Nicolayevich Vedenyapin – his Uncle Kolya. Uncle Kolya was a serious, religious man. He was concerned with the political ideas of his time and was looking for a new path that would change the world. In the future, he would write several important books that guided the thinking of many people during Russia's coming revolutionary years. Yury loved and admired this uncle who was now mother and father to him. The young boy listened to his Christian philosophy and accepted it as his own.

Chapter 2   Summer, 1903

Yury spent several happy years with Uncle Kolya, often travelling with him, and always listening to his ideas about Russia and about the role of the individual in society. On one of their trips they went to Duplyanka. They were going to a beautiful, large estate which reminded Yury of his mother. She had been fond of nature and had often taken him on long walks in the countryside. At the farm, Uncle Kolya spent the time discussing changes in the agricultural system with a fellow author, and Yury wandered around, listening to the birds and praying for his mother: 'Angel of God, lead me in the way of truth and tell Mama that I'm all right. She must not worry. If there is life after death, O Lord, please receive me. And please protect and keep dear Mama.' At this point Yury was suddenly overtaken with emotion and was not conscious of where he was for several minutes. When he shook himself awake, Yury thought of his father. He had forgotten to pray for him. 'He can wait,' he almost thought. It was difficult for the boy to pray for a father he did not remember at all.

While this was going on at the farm, a train was coming towards Duplyanka. One of the people on the train was Misha Gordon, an eleven-year-old boy who was travelling to Moscow with his father, a lawyer from Orenburg. One day in the near future, Yury and Misha would become friends, but on this day, they were still unknown to each other.

On this same train, there was another well-known lawyer and his client. The lawyer was Victor Ippolitovich Komarovsky and his client was the famous Zhivago, Yury's father. Zhivago had been in the Gordons' railway carriage for much of the journey. He had talked for hours to Misha's father about his financial matters. From time to time, the lawyer, Komarovsky, would find Zhivago and take him back to the bar for more drinks. It was easy to see that Zhivago's worries and his nervous condition were in some way to Komarovsky's advantage.

After one of these trips to the bar, Zhivago rushed into their car, grabbed Mr Gordon by the hand and then ran to the door and leapt from the train. He died at the exact moment that Yury forgot to pray for him. The train stopped in the valley near Duplyanka, but it was many years before Yury knew the whole story of his father's suicide.

Soon after this trip, Uncle Kolya sent Yury to Moscow to live with some distant relations, the Gromeko family. Yury was very happy in the Gromeko house. Both of the parents were kind and well educated, and their daughter, Tonya, became Yury's closest friend almost immediately. With the Gromekos, Yury enjoyed the kind of life that society believed was proper for a Zhivago.

Chapter 3   1905

In another part of Moscow, another young person was living a very different style of life from Yury's. Larissa Fyodorovna Guishar and her brother lived in three small rooms at the back of their mother's shop. The workers in the shop made dresses for the rich ladies of Moscow. Amalia, Larissa's mother, was a widow with a small amount of money. She was a frightened, weak woman who relied on an old friend of her husband's for advice. The friend was the handsome, confident lawyer who had been Zhivago's advisor: Victor Ippolitovich Komarovsky.

Komarovsky marched through the shop quite frequently with his fashionable beard and expensive clothes. He looked down his fine nose at the poor workers, and they whispered behind his back: 'Here comes Amalia's Don Juan.' 'The old devil.' 'The king of hearts!' They knew he was not good for Amalia, but their opinions did not matter.

Larissa, or Lara as she was usually called, was a natural beauty. She worked very hard at school and helped her mother as much as she could. It was easy to love her because she was the purest, kindest girl in the world. At sixteen, she understood her mother's fears about becoming poor, but she was strong and naturally optimistic. She had no worries about the future. Sadly, Komarovsky was to change her picture of herself and of her future.

One evening, Lara's mother, Amalia, had an appointment to go to a fashionable party with Komarovsky, but she felt ill and unable to go. Instead, she encouraged Komarovsky to take Lara. Komarovsky introduced Lara as his niece, but after several elegant evenings in the finest restaurants and clubs of the city, the ladies and gentlemen of Moscow society knew that Lara was something very different from a niece.

Lara could not control the events in her life. At first she went to places with Komarovsky because he was kind to her mother, and every evening with him was exciting – full of luxury and temptation. She floated along in a dream and did what Komarovsky wanted her to do. But when she was at home again and looked at herself in the mirror, Lara hated the woman that she saw. She knew that Komarovsky was evil and that he had made her evil, too. She wanted to be innocent again, but she could not break away from Komarovsky's power.

Lara's shame was her secret. Her mother must never know the awful truth about her and Komarovsky, and her friends at school would not understand or accept her double life. Her best friend was a boy named Pavel Pavlovich Antipov, known to everyone as Pasha. His father was a railway worker who was in jail because of his part in a railway strike and his mother was very ill in hospital.

*Every evening with Komarovsky was exciting – full of luxury
and temptation. She floated along in a dream and did
what Komarovsky wanted her to do.*

Pasha was now living with some of Lara's neighbours. He was a
charming young man – intelligent, funny, kind – and, because of
his father, he was involved with the politics of the day. Like many
students of that time, he wanted change in Russia, and he was
willing to work to make things better. But the centre of Pasha's
life was Lara. He loved her with his whole heart and would do
anything for her. Secretly, he had promised his life to her.

During this revolutionary time in Russia, many groups of
workers in Moscow, such as the railwaymen, went on strike.
Workers and students marched in the streets, hoping to change

conditions for everyone, but especially for the workers and the farmers. Then on October 17th, there was good news: the Tsar,* Nicholas II, had signed an agreement which would give land to the peasants and would make everyone in Russia equal. Unfortunately, the agreement was not worth the paper it was written on. Conditions for workers and farmers grew worse and worse. Students, politicians and churchmen wondered what would happen to their country. Some thought a lot about the situation and discussed it for hours and hours, while others looked for more direct ways to change their history. Pasha and his friends were among the groups of students and workers who were willing to fight on the streets for a new Russia.

One day, Amalia Guishar's workers surprised her when they stopped working and walked out of the shop. Amalia did not understand that the strike was not against her, but against a whole unfair system. She was depressed and worried and felt that she could not make sense of the world. Fortunately, she had a friend and neighbour who she could talk to. He was Tishkevich, a violinist, and he listened patiently to Amalia's concerns about her finances and her worries about Komarovsky.

Chapter 4   January, 1906

Many of Moscow's workers were now on strike, and, like Amalia Guishar, they wondered what would happen to their families and future. But in some parts of the city, people were still untouched by the troubles.

Behind the closed doors of their large, comfortable house, the Gromekos were planning one of their celebrated musical evenings. Everyone in the family was a great music lover. The

---

* Words with a star next to them are explained in the 'Historical notes' on page vi

preparations went on for days before the party. Carpets and curtains were cleaned, the furniture was moved around, and, in the kitchen, everyone was busy preparing bread, salads, meat, vegetables, pies and cakes for the elegant supper after the concert.

On the evening itself, Moscow's most important and fashionable ladies and gentlemen sat down to enjoy a special musical event. The musicians were the best in the city, but the music was dry and boring, and the songs seemed extremely long. The audience wished that the entertainment would stop so that they could go into supper.

Yury was sitting with Tonya and Misha Gordon – the three of them were always together in those days. Yury noticed that one of the servants was waving at Tonya's father. Gromeko tried to ignore the girl's signals, but she wouldn't stop waving and pointing. Finally, he walked quietly out of the room.

'Well, what is it? Why have you dragged me away from my guests?'

'I'm sorry, sir, but there is a man outside for Mr Tishkevich, one of the violinists. He says it's a matter of life or death. He must go immediately.'

'That's impossible. He'll have to wait until the end of this piece of music.'

'But, sir, someone is dying,' insisted the girl.

Alexander Gromeko returned to his guests, 'Ladies and gentlemen. Please forgive me, but I must end this wonderful music. Mr Tishkevich has had some bad news from home and must leave. I'll take him there myself. Please stay and enjoy yourselves. I will return very soon.'

It was an extremely cold night and Yury and Misha decided to go with Mr Gromeko and Tishkevich. The violinist's friend, Amalia Guishar, had tried to poison herself. Life had become a heavy weight for Amalia. With the shop closed, she had very little money, and now she was confused about her daughter and

Komarovsky. What was going on? What had changed? She was too frightened to face them directly, but she knew that something was wrong. The atmosphere felt dangerous when Lara and Komarovsky were in the same room. Amalia was not strong enough to find any solutions – instead, she drank poison.

Now the doctor was cleaning out her stomach and Tishkevich and Mr Gromeko were standing beside her bed. 'Mr Tishkevich, my dear, where's your hand? Please, give me your hand. I was such a fool. Oh, my imagination! But, now I see that everything is all right. And, here I am. Alive! Oh, forgive me, please, Tishkevich.'

'Be quiet now, Amalia. You have said enough. How awful! Mr Gromeko, I am sorry.'

'Don't worry, Tishkevich,' answered Gromeko, 'we'll leave now.'

All this time, Yury and Misha had been watching. They stared at the feverish woman, covered in sweat and talking wildly. This was a world they did not know. As they were leaving, they went through a small sitting-room. The walls were covered with photographs, and there were books, newspapers and fashion magazines piled high on the desk and table. Beyond the round table, in the soft light, they could see a girl of their own age, asleep in a big chair. She was completely exhausted and had slept through all of the noise and comings and goings.

'We'll leave now,' Gromeko said again, 'as soon as Mr Tishkevich comes out . . . I must say good night to him.'

But it was not Tishkevich who came into the room. It was a handsome, rather heavy, self-confident man. He was carrying a lamp which he placed on the table. The light woke up the sleeping girl and left Yury and Misha in dark shadows. The girl stretched and smiled up at the man.

On seeing this stranger, Misha pulled at Yury's sleeve and tried to tell him something. Yury told his friend to be quiet and stood very still, carefully watching the action before his eyes.

The girl and the man believed that they were alone. Not a word passed their lips, only their eyes met. But the understanding between them was complete, as if he were the master and she were a willing slave. His smile told her everything: the crisis was finished, the problem had disappeared. She looked at him and nodded contentedly – she understood that her mother's suicide attempt had failed, but that their secret was still safe.

Yury and Misha watched this show with horror. Misha was upset because he recognised the man. It was Komarovsky, the lawyer who had been with Yury's father when he committed suicide. He wanted to take Yury outside and explain who Komarovsky was. But Yury was trying to understand what he was watching. He stood in the darkness and stared at the two people in the circle of light. The girl was young and beautiful – like him and his friends – but she was controlled by this dangerous man. He knew that he was watching something forbidden, something which was wrong. The relationship between the man and the girl made Yury feel uncomfortable. His heart was painfully crowded with new feelings. He wanted to rescue the girl, but he could see that it was impossible for him to interfere. However, a connection now existed, and one day this girl, Lara Fyodorovna Guishar, would be the most important person in Yury's life. For now, she was still an upsetting mystery and someone who did not even know that Yury existed.

Misha pulled Yury outside and shouted, 'Do you know who that man is? Yury! He's the lawyer who made your father drink so much. He caused your father's death. He was on the train that day with your father. Remember, I told you!' But Yury was thinking about the girl and the future, not about his father and the past. He wasn't even sure what Misha was talking about. He wasn't sure about anything as they drove home through the frozen streets of Moscow.

Chapter 5   Christmas, 1911

Yury, Tonya and Misha were in their last term at university. In the spring they would all graduate: Yury in medicine, because he wanted to do something useful with his life, Misha in philosophy and Tonya in law. They were all very intelligent and hoped to succeed in their professions. A large part of their view of the world had come from Uncle Kolya's books. His ideas guided their thinking about history, politics and art, but especially about each individual being responsible for his or her own thoughts and actions.

Yury thought well and wrote even better. Since his school days, he had dreamed of writing a book about his impressions of life, but he didn't want to say things directly, he wanted to keep the most important things hidden under the surface, waiting for the intelligent reader to discover them. He was too young to write this book yet, so, instead, he wrote poems. These were practice for writing his great book one day.

The young people had very few worries, but they were concerned about Tonya's mother, Anna Ivanovna Gromeko. She was not well and had spent all of November and December of that year in bed. She often called Yury and Tonya to her side and talked to them about her family and her childhood at Varykino, her grandparents' enormous estate near the town of Yuryatin, far away in the Ural mountains.

On the 27th of December, Yury and Tonya were wondering if they should go to the Sventitskys' annual Christmas party that night. It was always the best party of the season and everyone would be there, but they did not want to be away from Tonya's mother. Anna was feeling a little better that day, and she called Yury, soon to be a doctor, to come to her bedroom and check her condition. Yury agreed that Anna seemed better, and so he stayed to talk with her.

'I want a word with you, Yury,' Anna said seriously.

'I know, Anna Ivanovna. You've seen the letter from the lawyers about my father's estate.'

'Yes, I have, and I want you to do the right thing. Do not act quickly. Think about your future.'

'I know you agree with Uncle Kolya, but, please, let me explain. The lawyers will take any money that my father left. There is no land, there are no factories, no houses. My father lost everything. I do not wish to go to court and listen to the details of his sad, foolish life, and still have nothing from him.'

'There are other people who will step forward if you do not want the estate,' protested Anna.

'Yes, I know. When Mama was still alive, my father fell in love with a strange princess, and she had a son by him. His name is Yevgraf and he's ten years old. I've seen a photograph of their house in the Urals. Sometimes I dream about it and feel that the windows are staring at me, giving me the evil eye. No! I don't want anything to do with this princess, her house or my father's pennies.'

'All right, Yury. I will leave that decision to you, but I will decide about tonight. You and Tonya must go to the Sventitskys' party. I am much better today, and I want to see you both in your evening clothes before you go out.'

◆

In the spring of 1906, Lara was in her final year at secondary school, but she was having a very difficult time. The relationship with Komarovsky had started six months earlier, and, at times, Lara believed that she was going insane. She was exhausted by late nights and by worrying. She hated herself for being weak, for acting like Komarovsky's slave, but she could not stay away from him.

Finally, Lara decided that she could not continue with a life which disgusted her. At school, she wrote a note to her best friend, Nadya Kologrivova: 'Nadya, I want to live away from Mother. Can you help me? I want a teaching job. I need to earn enough money to live independently. You know lots of rich people. Do you have any ideas?'

Nadya wrote back: 'Mother and Father are looking for a teacher for my little sister, Lipa. Why not come to us? It would be wonderful! You know we are all very fond of you.'

And so, Lara escaped from the terrible dream world that Komarovsky had trapped her in. She spent some years at Nadya's house where she was not only useful, but also greatly loved as a member of the family. She was able to save some money, because she was paid a very reasonable wage as Lipa's teacher, and she was also able to continue her own education. Nadya's parents were very kind and generous and helped Lara to solve another difficult problem while she lived with them.

One day in 1911, with no warning, Lara's brother, Rodya, arrived at the Kologrivovs' house. He was a student at a fashionable army college. He was both proud and stupid, and now he was in deep trouble because of gambling debts. He had gone to Komarovsky about his trouble, and the smooth lawyer was willing to help him if Lara wished him to. She had only to speak to Komarovsky and he would save her brother from disaster. Lara could not believe her ears. Her years of honest work for nothing! She did not think, she went straight to Nadya's father, and he helped her brother without question. But, before he left, Lara made Rodya give her his gun because he had threatened to shoot himself if he didn't get the money he needed. After he was gone, Lara's anger died, but she remained very upset.

Lara believed that she was in an impossible situation. Lipa was finished with school and did not need her any more, and she could not pay back the money she had borrowed from Nadya's father for Rodya's debts. She felt that she was not wanted any longer in the Kologrivov house, although this was not true. The family thought of her as a daughter and would have been very upset if they had known about Lara's concerns. In desperation, Lara came up with a crazy plan: she would go to Komarovsky and demand enough money from him to rent her own flat and to finish her studies. If he wouldn't help her, she would shoot him with her brother's gun. On December 27th, she left Nadya's house to look for him. She hid the gun in her coat.

As Lara walked through the snow, Tonya and Yury were in Anna Ivanovna's bedroom, showing her how fine they looked before they left for the Sventitskys' party. Anna was very happy to see her two favourite young people.

'Oh, my goodness. Where is my little Yury? And my sweet Tonya? What has happened to my children? You are both grown up now, ready to face the world on your own. Come here, let me look at you.' They came closer for Anna Ivanovna to see them and stood shoulder to shoulder beside her bed.

'Tonya, you are beautiful, perfect. And Yury, so handsome and elegant. My heart is very happy tonight. You are ready for the best, the brightest party of the year. I think you are ready for the world. Listen to me ...,' but she was interrupted by her own coughs. Yury and Tonya reached out to her and their hands touched. Still coughing, Anna held their hands in hers and said, 'If I die, stay together. You are meant for each other. Get married. There now, you are an official couple,' and she began to cry softly. 'Now, go. You must enjoy the party for me.'

On the way to the Sventitskys' house, Tonya and Yury were changed people. After six years as children and young adults together, they knew everything about each other. They loved to study together and argue about politics and religion. They shared the same taste in art and literature and laughed at the same jokes. They were part of the same close, loving family, but suddenly there was something new between them. Now they looked at each other with different eyes. They were a man and a woman and saw that they were truly, deeply in love with each other. For both of them, it was as if Tonya's mother had opened a secret door and had shown them a bright, magic future.

They arrived at the party and were greeted by the Sventitskys and many other old friends. There was dancing for the young people, card-playing and a little gambling for their elders, and tables full of every description of Christmas food and drink. Everyone was in evening dress and looked as if they were enjoying the party atmosphere. Everyone, that is, but one young lady: Lara. She had learned that Komarovsky was at the Sventitskys' party, and she was searching for him with a desperate look in her eye. She danced with a young man she knew from university and continued her search. Suddenly she saw Komarovsky at a card table, pulled out the gun and fired at him.

Everyone turned and looked in the direction of the sound. There was a moment's silence, and then people began screaming and running towards the injured man. 'What has she done? What has she done?' Komarovsky kept saying. He was not hurt. The shot had hit another man, but he knew it had been meant for him.

Yury hurried over to the injured man and saw Lara and Komarovsky for the second time. That girl! Again in a sensational situation! And that evil man! But Yury had no time to think about Lara and Komarovsky. Tonya rushed over to him – they were needed at home immediately. Yury forgot everything else and ran out of the house with Tonya.

They did not find Anna Ivanovna alive. When they ran up the stairs to her room she had been dead for ten minutes. Anna's death was a tragedy for the whole family, but Tonya, especially, was beside herself with sadness. Yury remembered the pure terror he had felt ten years earlier when his dear mother had died. Now he was afraid of nothing, neither of life nor death. He had learnt

*Suddenly Lara saw Komarovsky at a card table, pulled out the
gun and fired at him.*

many things in the last ten years – from literature, art, history, the Bible – and felt that he now understood himself and his world. He would help Tonya. He would protect her and stay beside her always, and he would write a poem for her mother so that they would never forget her.

◆

After the guests had left the Christmas party, Lara lay feverish and half conscious in one of the Sventitskys' bedrooms. The rest of the house was dark and quiet, but one nervous, angry person was still awake, trying to decide on his next course of action. Komarovsky's good name was threatened, and he was determined to stop any gossip that might link him to Lara or to the shooting. He had already spoken to the police and tried to smooth things over. He must not go to court and answer questions about his private life. He would find a place for Lara to live – anything to keep her quiet and out of his way. And, above all, he would never go near her. When he looked at her, he had to admit that she was still extremely attractive to him. She was intelligent and beautiful but wild at the same time. He had always known that she was special, and he wanted her desperately. But now he could see that she had the power to destroy him. He would help her and then try to forget her.

Chapter 6   1915, During World War I

Soon Lara was living in her own flat and spending her time at the university or with Pasha. Mr Kologrivov, Nadya's father, had helped her with some extra money, and both Lara and Pasha would graduate from university soon. Their dream was to get married, move out of Moscow, and then work in the country as teachers. Secretly, Lara was afraid that Komarovsky – or at least her past relationship with him – would spoil their dream. She tried to protect Pasha from her dark secrets, but he believed that nothing could damage his love for Lara. They got married soon afterwards and moved to Yuryatin, the small town in the Urals where Lara had been born and had spent her childhood.

By this time, Yury and Tonya were also married. Yury was a doctor at a big Moscow hospital, and, as in most hospitals at that time, the beds were full of injured soldiers from the battlefields. But in the autumn of 1915, Yury was more concerned about Tonya. She was in hospital, waiting for the birth of their first baby. She had been there for three days before Yury finally heard the news. A nurse found him, 'Congratulations. It's a son. Be very loving and gentle with your wife. She has had a bad time.'

'She's safe. Tonya and the baby are safe,' Yury said, almost as a prayer. The great thing was that Tonya was no longer in danger. She was fine and they were parents.

◆

Lara and Pasha had now been in Yuryatin for four years. Lara had her hands full and plenty to think about. She took care of their house and their daughter, Katya, who was three years old. She was also a teacher at the girls' high school and shared all of Pasha's interests, too. She worked constantly, but she was very content. This was exactly the life she had dreamed of. She was happy to be in Yuryatin once again with people who knew her and her family. She liked these people and their simple way of life.

Pasha was also a teacher, but teaching and family life were not enough for him. He missed the big city and sometimes criticised the people of Yuryatin rather strongly. He thought that their ideas, especially their political ideas, were very simple. He stayed away from the local people and, instead, concentrated on his education. He could read quickly and remembered almost everything he read. He was a teacher of Latin and Ancient

History, and now he taught himself everything he could about science, physics and mathematics. He sank himself into studying, often forgetting to eat or sleep. And the more he learned, the less he liked living in Yuryatin.

Pasha and Lara's relationship was good but not perfect. They loved each other very deeply, but they were not able to be completely natural with each other. Pasha knew about Komarovsky and worried that Lara believed he thought badly of her because of her past. Lara tried to be kind and loving, but sometimes she was too much like a mother in Pasha's eyes. They were often too polite to each other, too careful, which made things more complicated.

One night when he could not sleep, Pasha stood alone, staring into the night. He questioned Lara's love for him, and then even wondered if his love for her was really true. He began to think that they were acting roles instead of behaving honestly. And yet, he couldn't hurt Lara; she meant everything to him. He looked up at the stars as if searching for a solution. What should he do? Suddenly an army train came into view and went hurrying past to the west. Pasha smiled, got up and returned to bed. He had found his answer.

When Pasha told Lara about his decision, she could not believe her ears. He had arranged everything and was leaving for the army school in Omsk. 'Pasha, Pasha, darling,' screamed Lara, 'don't leave us! What's the matter with you? You are not my Pasha. What has changed you? You don't even respect soldiers.'

Suddenly, she realised that her husband didn't actually want to be in the army – he wanted to be away from her. She didn't understand completely, but she knew that he misunderstood her love for him. She became silent and helped him to pack his things.

Lara's whole life seemed silent without her husband. Her brightest hopes and dreams had drifted away. But eventually Pasha wrote from the battlefield and sounded less depressed. He wanted to be with Lara and Katya and prayed for an opportunity to visit his home in Yuryatin. But then his letters stopped and Lara could not get any news about him. She was filled with worry so she took action. She trained as a nurse and went to look for Pasha in the war. She left Katya with her old student, Lipa, in Moscow and got a job as a nurse on a hospital train going to the Hungarian border and passing through the town of Liski, the last address she had had from Pasha.

Lara didn't know yet, but the news about her husband was not good. During a very fierce battle, Pasha had led an attack against the Austrians. He and his men had moved quickly forwards across an open field towards the enemy. Suddenly, the big German guns opened fire on them. Black clouds of smoke hid the soldiers, but the observers behind them believed that all of the Russian soldiers were dead.

Chapter 7   Winter, 1916

Misha Gordon was travelling by train from Moscow to the war front to see his childhood friend, Dr Yury Andreyevich Zhivago. Yury was working in one of the army's hospitals. The train passed villages that the enemy had destroyed. Old people looked up at the train, wondering when peace and order would return to their lives.

Misha finally found Yury and spent a week with him at the hospital. They talked about everything in the world, just like they had done when they were students. Yury couldn't accept the horrors caused by a modern war. Men's bodies were torn to pieces, but sometimes they didn't die. These men became Yury's patients. How could people be so cruel to each other? They talked about the spirit of the times, the impossible role of the Tsar and of the suffering of Jewish people in their own country. Yury did not understand how one group of Russians could hate another group of their own countrymen.

The following day, Yury came back to their living area and said, 'We're all leaving here. All of the medical people have received orders to move out. I don't know where we're going to.'

They both packed that afternoon without any rush. During the night they were awakened by shouts, the sound of guns and men running. The Germans had broken through and were attacking the village. The hospital had to be moved immediately.

'We'll all be gone before dawn,' Yury told Misha. 'You'll go with the first group. I've told them to wait for you. Hurry up! I'll come with you and get you a seat.'

'What are you going to do?' asked Misha.

'I'll come with the second group. Don't worry. I have to go back and collect my medical equipment first.'

They separated at the edge of the village. Yury waved to Misha and then hurried back to the hospital. He had almost reached the hospital building when he was knocked down by the force of an explosion. He fell in the middle of the road, bleeding and unconscious.

Chapter 8   1917

Yury was recovering in the army hospital in a small forgotten town. It was a warm day at the end of February. The window near his bed was open, and he was reading letters from Tonya that had just been delivered to him. All of the patients were bored and waiting for their dinners.

Suddenly everyone's attention was caught by the sound of light footsteps coming into the large room. Lara, or Nurse Antipova, walked into the room and greeted the men. Yury recognised her at once and so did one other patient.

'Larissa Fyodorovna Antipova!' said the other man, 'I knew your husband. We were officers together for almost a year. I've kept his things for you.'

'It isn't possible,' Lara kept saying. 'Who are you? Please, tell me how my husband died. What happened? Please don't be afraid to tell me.'

'I am Iosif Gimazetdinovich Galiullin. I know you, Larissa Fyodorovna, from Moscow. I lived near you in 1905 on Brest Street.'

'I'm sorry, I don't remember you, but, goodness me, I remember that year. How extraordinary! But, Pasha. Please tell me about my dear Pasha.'

Galiullin told Lara what had happened to her husband and then she left the room very quietly in tears. Yury thought about the two times he had seen her: once as a schoolgirl when her mother had tried to commit suicide and once when she had shot a man at a Christmas party. By the time Lara returned to the room, Yury had decided not to mention these events and upset her further. When she spoke to him, he said, 'Thank you for your help. I am a doctor. I am looking after myself. I don't need anything.'

'Why should he seem so offended?' Lara wondered. But, as the days passed, she talked to Yury as she talked to each of her patients, and she got to know him a bit better. 'What a curious man. Young and serious, not exactly handsome, but intelligent, with a very attractive character. However, it's not my business. My business is to finish my job here as soon as possible and get back to Katya, and then back to Yuryatin and our life there. Now that I no longer have Pasha, I must be strong for my poor daughter.'

Yury's head was full of some news from Moscow. He had heard that Misha and some other friends had produced his book; it had impressed many people, and his ideas were taken seriously. Moscow was going through exciting times. The Russian people

Yury and Lara were often brought together by their work.
They became sincere friends.

were growing more and more discontented. A serious political
event seemed to be just around the corner. Yury's dreams – both
awake and asleep – were about Moscow, about his work, about
the political situation and about Tonya and Sasha.

Yury woke up from his dreams because of the noise of other
patients running in from other rooms. They were all shouting,
'Street fighting in Petersburg! The soldiers have joined the rebels!
It's the Revolution!'*

◆

The patients and staff from the hospital were moved to the small
town of Melyuzeyevo. Dr Zhivago, Nurse Antipova and
Galiullin, the officer who had been with Pasha, were considered
to be experienced and clever because they were from Moscow.
They were picked for every job, but all three dreamed of the day
when they could return to their families and their ordinary
jobs. Yury and Lara were often brought together by their work.
They became sincere friends and learned to respect each other's
talents and hard work.

When Yury had any free time, he wrote letters to Tonya.

Darling Tonya,

. . . I've been to see some of the soldiers in the neighbourhood. There is an impression of confusion and desperation everywhere.

Have I told you that I do a lot of work with a certain Antipova, a nurse from Moscow who was born in the Urals? Do you remember the girl student who shot a man at that terrible party on the night your mother died? And, Misha and I once saw her in a poor district of Moscow – your father took Misha and me to her flat because of a suicide attempt. Well, that girl was Antipova.

I keep trying to get home, but it is very difficult. The problem is not the work here really, anyone could do it – but it's impossible to arrange a journey. Either there are no trains or they are completely full and don't even stop here. Of course, this situation can't last forever. Antipova, Galiullin and I are all determined to leave next week. We'll go separately, so we will each have a better chance. So, I might surprise you one day, but I'll try to send you a telegram.

All my love,
Yury

Before he left, he received Tonya's reply. Her words were marked with tears, and she begged him not to come back to Moscow but to go straight to the Urals with the wonderful Nurse Antipova. Tonya believed that her simple ways must look dull compared to Lara's many sensational adventures. She had persuaded herself that Yury was in love with Lara, and that she had been forgotten.

Yury wrote back to his wife immediately. 'You are out of your mind, Tonya! How could you imagine such a thing? Don't you feel my love for you? If it were not for you and for my faithful thoughts of you and our home, I would have died before now. But words are useless. Soon we will be together and our life will begin again. Tonya, you are everything to me. Please do not forget that.'

Throughout the district around Melyuzeyevo, people were feeling the effects of the revolution. A neighbouring town attempted to become independent from the central government. They were led by an extraordinary man with ideas from the 1905 revolution. The people wanted to share all of the work and to divide the land equally. But their independence lasted only a fortnight. Then the Provisional Government was in charge of the town again.

Finally, there was news of more trains and Lara made her plans to leave Melyuzeyevo. Yury found her in the laundry room and told her that he needed to talk to her. She talked about the revolution and about all the problems involved with leaving, but Yury wanted to talk about his feelings for her. He had been analysing these feelings since he received Tonya's letter.

'I want to tell you about my wife, and my son, and myself . . . Tell me, why can't an adult man talk to an adult woman without everyone thinking that they are more than friends? Don't answer – just let me talk.

'The world has been turned upside down. It was partly the war, and then the revolution did the rest. Suddenly everyone was free, free to create themselves as new people. It's as if there were two revolutions: a personal revolution for each of us as well as the general one. Now, people intend to experience a new life, not in books and pictures, not in theory, but in practice.'

Lara gave him a serious look, but Yury rushed on, saying everything that came into his head.

'I want an honest life. I want to work hard and be a part of the great changes in our country. I get very excited about what is going on all around us, and then I see you. You look sad and lost and my heart aches for you. I'd give up anything to know that you are all right. I wish that someone close to you – your husband or your best friend – would come and tell me to stop worrying about you and to leave you alone. But, of course, then I'd knock him down. . . . Sorry, I didn't mean that.'

Yury had surprised himself as well as Lara. He was embarrassed and walked to the window so that he didn't have to see Lara looking at him.

'I was afraid of this,' Lara said softly, as if to herself. 'I shouldn't have ... if only ...Yury Andreyevich, you must be sensible. Go outside and get some fresh air, and then come back, my dear, and be as I've known you until now, and as I want you to be. Do you hear, Yury? I know you can do it. Please, for me, I beg you to.'

They had no more discussions of this kind, and a week later Lara left.

Soon after, Dr Yury Andreyevich Zhivago also set off for home. Friends helped him to find a seat on a train for Moscow, and he had time to think. His thoughts moved in two big circles, constantly changing shape and confusing him.

In one circle were his thoughts of Tonya, their son and their home with its warmth, sincerity and love. After more than two years away from Moscow, he dreamed of being there and having his family safe and whole again.

This circle also contained his commitment to the revolution, as he understood it, and his excitement about a new future for Russia. He was eager to talk to his friends in Moscow and to Uncle Kolya about new ideas in philosophy, art and politics.

The other circle also contained new ideas, but they were very different from the ideas in the first circle. It contained his memories of the war: blood, terror and cruelty. He worried about the side of the revolution that was being led by professionals, and about the peasants who were being stepped on and forgotten.

Among these new thoughts, he saw Nurse Antipova, Lara, living in the Urals with her daughter. She was mysterious and strong, but was she strong enough to make a life for the two of them in the middle of a revolution? Yury wanted to be near her, he wanted to be the man that she could rely on. But, at the same time, he wanted to stop himself from loving her; he had to stop thinking about her.

Following a restless night, Yury looked out of the train and recognised where he was and what was waiting for him. After almost three years of war and struggle, coming home had become his purpose in life – coming home to his family, to himself, to a new life. Suddenly, he saw the church of Christ the Saviour over the top of a hill, then the chimneys, roofs and houses of the city.

'Moscow,' said Yury. 'It's time to get ready.'

♦

Yury was able to hire a carriage at the station, and as he looked at the streets of Moscow during his ride home, he saw a picture of what the city would soon become. The markets were closed because there was nothing to buy or sell, the streets were dirty because no one cleaned them, and thin, hopeless old people stood beside the buildings, trying to sell useless, but once expensive objects from their past because they needed a few pennies to buy bread.

The carriage came close to Yury's house and he felt his heart begin to beat faster in his chest. He ran up the steps to his front door and rang the bell. Suddenly, Tonya appeared and they rushed into each other's arms. A moment later they were both talking at once.

'First of all, is everybody well?' asked Yury.

'Yes, don't worry, but Yury, listen. I wrote a lot of silly nonsense in one letter. You must forgive me. You're home now, and we're together. That's all that matters.'

'Tonya, darling, you have always been the only woman in my life and in my heart. No more of this talk. How young you look, and so pretty! And where is Sasha? How is he?'

'All right, thank God. He's just woken up. We'll see him in a minute.'

'And your father? Is he at home?' asked Yury.

26

'No, of course not. Didn't you get my last letter? Father is at the city offices from morning to night. He's the chief official from this district. Can you believe it?'

Tonya led Yury up the back stairs. 'Don't we go through the sitting-room any more?' Yury wanted to know.

'Well, you see, Yury, we gave part of the ground floor to the Agricultural Academy and the top floor as well. We are using three rooms upstairs for ourselves. It's better that way, don't you agree?'

'Yes, definitely. There really was something unhealthy in the way rich people used to live. Too much furniture, too many rooms, too much concern about the individual. I'm glad we're sharing what we have. But still, I don't think all of these changes will be easy for anyone.'

'Oh, Yury,' interrupted Tonya, 'I've got wonderful news for you. Nikolay Nikolayevich is back.'

'Uncle Kolya?! Are you serious? Where is he now?'

'Calm down. He's in the country – he'll be back tomorrow. He and father constantly argue about politics. But, there are more urgent topics to discuss. We hear rumours every day: they say there won't be any fuel for heat, or any water or light. They say the new government will get rid of money. Nothing will be coming into the city. We need to plan for the winter.'

'We will, Tonya. We'll get through it. And, what about all of our friends? What is everyone doing these days?'

Yury continued to ask questions, and Tonya told him about their friends and about the exciting but hard life they were all facing now. But in all of this excitement, the most important event for Yury was meeting his son. Yury had been called into the army almost immediately after Sasha was born, so that he hardly knew his little boy. He was filled with emotion as he walked into the room where Sasha was waiting.

Little Sasha let the stranger get quite close to him, then he jumped into his mother's arms and slapped Yury's face. He had frightened himself with this bold action and burst into sad, confused tears.

'Sasha, what will Daddy think?' Tonya shouted at the poor little boy. 'He'll think Sasha is a bad boy. Now, kiss Daddy. Don't cry, silly.'

'Don't worry, Tonya,' said Yury calmly. 'Don't upset him. It's so natural. The boy has never seen me. Tomorrow he'll have a good look at me and then we'll be friends. We'll get along wonderfully.' And yet, Yury left the room feeling cold and depressed. Was his son's reaction a sign of what the future would be like?

Over the next few days, Yury's depression did not lift. He began to realise how many changes had already taken place. Many of his old friends seemed dull and colourless. Without their large houses and lots of money in the bank, they didn't seem to have any real character or any original ideas. Yury was comfortable only with Tonya, her father, Uncle Kolya and two or three colleagues who were working at ordinary jobs which they did well and without complaining.

Yury's greatest pleasure was talking to Uncle Kolya again. On their first meeting they felt drunk with the excitement of seeing each other. They laughed and cried, threw their arms round each other and talked about everything they had done over the last two years, and about the present political situation. They were both bolshevik★ supporters and believed that a revolution had been necessary. Uncle Kolya argued that for centuries the common people had lived difficult, impossible lives. The great differences between the rich and the poor were not natural or fair. This had been known for a long time, and the world had been preparing for a great change – a change that would bring light to the people and put everything and everybody in their proper places. Both Yury and his uncle supported the principles of the revolution, but they worried about how the new system would work in people's day-to-day lives.

After they had discussed the great events, the two men calmed down and enjoyed something very special. They had an extraordinary relationship that went beyond being uncle and nephew, or being good citizens. They shared an understanding of what it means to be an artist. For ten years, Uncle Kolya had not talked to anyone about the problems of writing and the importance of a writer's work. But he could talk to Yury about these things, and they could understand each other completely and encourage each other. They would shout, rush up and down the room, shake their heads, stand in deep silence and then find a solution to some artistic problem they were discussing. For both men, being together again was like waking up after a long sleep and realising that they were fully alive.

◆

It was the autumn of 1917 and everyone was worried about getting through the coming winter and seeing another spring. People in Moscow were city people; in general, they were as helpless as children. And they were not familiar with going without food or heat.

Yury remained sane by concentrating on taking care of his family. He was back at his job at the Hospital of the Holy Cross, and although he was very excited about Russia's future, he tried to stay out of politics. He worked long hours and spent his free time fixing things at home, looking for food and fuel and sometimes writing poems.

One cold dark night, shortly before the October battles, Yury found a man lying unconscious on the pavement. The man had been attacked and robbed. Yury checked him carefully and sent him to the hospital in a carriage. Later he learned that the man was an important politician. From then on this man helped and protected the Zhivago family whenever he could. Without such help, it is not certain that the Zhivagos would have seen the next spring.

One Sunday afternoon in October, Uncle Kolya and Misha Gordon, Yury's old school friend, came rushing into the Zhivagos' living area in the big house. 'They're fighting in the streets. The bolsheviks are fighting against the soldiers from the Provisional Government.★ You can't get through Nikitsky Gate, you have to go round it. Come on, Yury,' shouted Uncle Kolya. 'Put your coat on and come outside. You've got to see it. This is history. Something like this happens only once in a lifetime.'

But Misha reported increasing gunfire. People had been shot in the street and all traffic had been stopped. They stayed in the house for three days and nights, waiting to see who would be in control. The city had stopped living until the victory was decided. At the end of three days, Yury and Tonya were exhausted by the endless discussion and, fortunately, Misha and Uncle Kolya felt that it was safe enough to leave.

It was still too early to say that Moscow was at peace, and several parts of the city remained closed, but Yury went out the next day to visit a colleague. The streets were almost empty, and Yury walked quickly through the light snow. Without warning, the light snow turned into a terrible storm. The wind whistled down the side streets and a blanket of snow quickly covered the whole city. To Yury, it seemed that there was something similar between the political events and the terrible weather.

A newsboy came running around a corner in front of Yury carrying a bunch of freshly printed newspapers under his arm and shouting, 'All the latest! Get the latest news!'

Yury ran after the boy and overtook him at the next corner. 'Keep the change,' said Yury, and then he found a lighted apartment entrance to stand in and read the latest news. The paper gave the official announcement from Petersburg that a Soviet of People's Commissars★ had been formed and that Soviet power and the Dictatorship of the Proletariat★ had been set up in

'They're fighting in the streets. The bolsheviks are fighting against the soldiers from the Provisional Government,' shouted Uncle Kolya.

Russia. After that, there were the first rules from the new government. Yury was shaken by the greatness of the moment and by the thought of its importance for centuries to come.

As he was reading the newspaper, Yury was interrupted by someone coming down the stairs of the apartment building. He looked up and saw a boy of about eighteen, in a reindeer cap and a stiff reindeer coat. The boy was dark and had narrow, Siberian eyes and a proud, handsome face. He looked at Yury as if he knew him, but he was too shy to speak. Yury gave the boy a cold, hard stare which frightened him away. How could Yury have known that at that moment he had been face to face with his half-brother, Yevgraf?

Within a few minutes, Yury had forgotten the boy. His mind was full of news, and he wanted to be at home and to tell Tonya and Gromeko what had happened to their country. They sat up most of that night, trying to make sense of these latest events. 'The surprise,' said Yury, 'is that our leaders have decided to create a new world in the middle of the old one. This new history must begin now, today, without any concern about what is already here. This is a great idea, but I doubt that it can work.'

The dark, cold, hungry winter of 1917–18 arrived, and the people of Moscow struggled to stay alive. The old way of life and the new ways did not fit together, but they tried to exist side by side. The Civil War,★ which caused so many new problems for the country, would not begin for almost another year. For now, there was the appointment of new people to run government departments for housing, industry, business and city services. The new leaders had unlimited power and spent their days making bolshevik rules for every part of life.

Yury's hospital changed from the Hospital of the Holy Cross to the Second Reformed Hospital. Many other things about the hospital changed, too. Some doctors were pushed out and others looked for unofficial ways to make more money outside the hospital. Yury stayed on but spent more and more of his time in meetings about the government's new plan for hospitals. If he had any free time, he was looking for potatoes to buy in order to feed his family.

Like most people around them, the Zhivagos were not healthy. They were cold most of the time, never had enough to eat and were always exhausted. Their politician friend helped them many times, but finally his circumstances were the same as everyone else's, and he had nothing extra to give away. There was typhus throughout the city, and, finally, one day Yury became one of its victims. He was returning home with fire wood and couldn't see properly. Then he couldn't walk in a straight line. 'This is it,' he thought. 'I'm finished, it's typhus.' Someone carried him home, but he had no idea what was going on around him for almost a fortnight.

When Yury was out of danger, he began to see a boy near his bed. The boy had narrow eyes and was wearing a reindeer cap. Yury thought he was the spirit of death, but how could 'death' help him write poems and bring him hot soup and bread? Finally, Yury really woke up from his black dream in which he had watched love win the battle against death.

Little by little he noticed that he was drinking tea with sugar in it and eating white bread with real butter. 'How did you get all of this?' he asked Tonya.

'Your brother got it for us.'

'My brother? What do you mean?'

'Well, yes, your half-brother Yevgraf from Tomsk. He came every day while you were ill. He took care of all of us,' Tonya explained.

'Does he wear a reindeer cap and a reindeer coat?'

'That's right. So you did see him. You were unconscious for days. He admires you very much. He has read everything you have written. And he brought us wonderful things: rice, dried

33

fruit, sugar. I think he has a connection with the new government. He's gone back to Tomsk now, and he thinks we should leave Moscow for a year or two. I suggested the Varykino estate, my Grandfather Krueger's place, and Yevgraf said it was a good idea. We could grow vegetables and hunt for food. What do you think, Yury?'

In April of 1918, Dr Zhivago left Moscow with his family. They were on their way to the Varykino estate, near the town of Yuryatin, far away in the Urals.

Chapter 9   1918

Leaving Moscow was not a simple operation. First of all, Yury was against the journey. 'What worries me,' he told Tonya and her father, 'is the complete uncertainty. We are leaving a place that we know and where we have a house and friends, to go to a place that we know nothing about. Who is in power in that part of the country? Who is living in your grandparents' house? Will we be allowed to live on the estate?'

In the end, Tonya and Gromeko won the argument. The situation in Moscow was getting worse, and Tonya believed that if they worked hard in the country they would have a better chance of fitting in with the new bolshevik system.

And so Yury began spending hours at the train station every day. He had to queue for tickets, for permission papers, for information about trains. But, finally the day came for the family to leave. As usual, the station was dirty and very crowded. There were many other families trying to leave the city, soldiers going to the battlefields to the east and typhus victims who had been pushed out of the hospitals before they were well. When the train came into the station, Yury fought his way through the crowd and found a corner with a window for his family. The train was packed with people and their boxes and baskets, all of which contained food and objects that they could use as money on the journey. There were twenty-three carriages and about six hundred people: the rich and poor, soldiers and sailors and men who had been forced to join labour gangs.

Whenever the train stopped, Tonya looked out and decided whether it was a good idea to get off or not. Her decision depended on the size of the station and the appearance of the people standing there. Would she be able to bargain with someone for fresh food for her family? At one large station, she combed her hair and found a beautifully decorated towel in her basket. Then she set off in search of food, carrying the towel across her shoulder.

Girls and women from the local villages were sitting beside the station office, selling fresh vegetables, cheese, meat and hot bread. The soldiers and sailors were the best customers, and the women enjoyed joking with them. At the end of the row of women, Tonya saw an old peasant wearing a black scarf. She waved to Tonya and whispered, 'Look at this. I bet you haven't seen one of these in a long time. You can have half of it for your towel.'

The woman showed Tonya a cooked duck – fat and juicy and just the thing for her family. She gave the woman her towel and felt a bit embarrassed. Had she cheated the woman or just made a good bargain?

There were several men travelling east for the labour gangs in each carriage, including the Zhivagos' carriage. One sixteen-year-old boy was particularly noticeable. Vassya Brykin was from the Vyatka district. His father had been killed in World War I, and his poor mother had sent him to Petersburg to live with his aunt and uncle and to work in his uncle's shop.

One day at the beginning of 1918, Vassya's uncle had been chosen by the new Labour Department for one of the labour gangs. His wife was very upset by this and was sure that a mistake had been made. She and Vassya went to the station to say goodbye to the uncle. He begged the guard for permission to leave the train and kiss his wife before the train left. The guard refused unless someone would stay on the train in his place, so the uncle offered Vassya. The boy was put inside the train and his uncle was let out. This was the last Vassya ever saw of his aunt and uncle.

When the trick was discovered, Vassya burst into tears and begged the guard to let him go, but it was no good. The guard had to report to his boss with a certain number of workers. That was how Vassya came to be in a labour gang.

Vassya was an attractive boy who looked like a young prince or an angel in an oil painting. He was unusually innocent and unspoilt. His favourite thing to do on the train was to sit on the floor and listen to the older people as they talked about their past adventures or the politics of the day. By watching his face, you could almost follow the conversation without hearing it.

The journey lasted for days and days, and the train travelled through many empty villages that had been destroyed by either the White or the Red Army.* One day, the train pulled into Lower Kelmes, a burnt out station with an empty village behind it. But there were still a few people around and the station master came out to talk to the train driver.

'It looks like you've had a fire,' said the driver.

'Yes, we certainly had a fire, but that wasn't the worst thing that happened,' answered the station master.

'I don't understand what you mean.'

'It's better not to try.'

'You don't mean Strelnikov!' said the driver.

'I do. And we hadn't done anything. Our neighbours in the next village refused to give their horses to the Red Army or to allow their young men to join the labour gangs.'

'I see. So their village was destroyed?'

'Naturally. And we were attacked and burnt out of our houses as insurance. Strelnikov won't have any more trouble in this district,' said the station master.

This was not the first time that the people on the train had heard the name Strelnikov. Like the citizens of Lower Kelmes, they began to link this name with the signs of violence that they saw.

As the journey continued, the passengers were often called on to help the train crew. Sometimes they got off the train and cleared snow from its path, at other times, they looked for wood and cut it to use as fuel for the engines. Yury and Gromeko enjoyed this occasional physical work after so much time on the train. It also gave them a chance to talk privately.

'Don't go so fast, you'll tire yourself,' Yury told his father-in-law. 'Let's have a rest and a talk. We've cut a lot of wood in a short time.'

'What do you want to talk about?' asked the older man.

'We're going deeper and deeper into a part of the country that is unfamiliar to us. These are revolutionary times – no one knows what to expect from one village to the next. Some villages have been completely destroyed, others are controlled by the Whites and still others by the Reds.'

'It's not what we expected, is it? Do you remember that night, in the middle of the big storm, when you brought home the paper with the first news of the new government? We were excited because it was so direct and honest. But no political system can stay pure, and now we see things happening that we cannot agree with,' said Gromeko.

'We must try to live according to the original ideas of the revolution. We're not going to the Varykino estate in order to be the owners. There are no owners these days. We'll live in the modern way. We'll plant our vegetables, look after a few animals and be good neighbours. But we must be very careful. We'll live a quiet life and try to keep our mouths shut.'

The two men went back to the train feeling a bit sad after their conversation, but they felt satisfied with the fact that they understood each other so well.

As spring came closer, it became hot and uncomfortable inside the train. Early one morning, they pulled into a big station and Yury carefully got down from his bed and opened the carriage door. Everyone else was still sleeping.

Yury could hear a sound, like distant thunder, but because of his experience in the war, he recognised the sound of guns. The train was near the battlefields.

'That's it, we're right at the battle front,' he nodded to himself as he jumped down from the carriage. He walked to the back of the train and saw that two carriages had been taken away. They had carried the soldiers; maybe they were already in the middle of the fighting.

Yury walked to the other end of the train. 'Where are you going? Do you have permission to be off the train?' a guard asked as he stopped Yury.

'What is this station?' Yury asked softly.

'Why do you need to know? Who are you?'

'I am a doctor from Moscow. My family and I are passengers on this train. Here are my papers.'

'I can't read your papers in this fog. Get back on the train while you're still in one piece,' warned the guard.

Yury walked down the other side of the train. Through the fog he could see some small boats and the shore of a river. Another guard appeared in front of him. 'Who gave you permission to wander around? What are you looking for?'

'What river is this?' Yury asked without thinking. He had decided earlier not to ask any more questions.

The second guard took Yury by the arm at the same time as the first guard appeared from the other side of the train. 'Is he still asking questions?'

'Yes. Do you know him?' asked the second guard.

'I saw him a few minutes ago. I suspect he's up to something. Get his papers. We'll take him to our train and see what the boss says.'

Yury was led away to a special train that was being used as the offices of the Red Army Commissar Strelnikov. He was left in a clean, comfortable carriage where tidy, well-dressed people were working. Yury was surprised by the business-like atmosphere; he had had a different picture in his mind of how Strelnikov, the terror of the region, would operate.

Yury was brought to this office and then forgotten. To the people around him, he wasn't there, although his papers lay on one of the desks. From little bits of conversation, Yury learned that they were very close to Yuryatin, and that the Whites were in charge of the region. The soldiers from the train were obviously much more important to these people than someone like Yury was.

Suddenly a man marched into the room. The force of his character filled the carriage, and Yury knew at once that this was Strelnikov. He seemed brilliant and original in every way – tall and handsome and alive with an extraordinary intelligence.

'Congratulations,' he said to his staff. 'We've driven the Whites out of Yuryatin. And who is this man?'

'We think he's the spy that we were looking for,' reported one of the guards.

'Nonsense! He's nothing like him. I apologise, Comrade. My guards have made a mistake. You're free to go. Where are this man's papers?' demanded Strelnikov. Then he saw Yury's name and his Moscow address. 'Ah … Zhivago … from Moscow. Please, come with me. I won't keep you long.'

Who was this Strelnikov? He had been born in Moscow, gone to university and then to a teaching job in the Urals with his wife. In the 1914–18 war, he had been captured, reported missing and believed killed. He had only recently escaped from prison in

Germany. He had returned to Russia with the spirit of the revolution shining in his eyes. He quickly became a leader because of two things: his power of clear and logical reasoning and his methods on the battlefield which were often harsh, but led to victories for the Reds.

'Zhivago,' repeated Strelnikov when they were sitting in his private room. 'Why are you going to Varykino? It's very rural for a doctor from Moscow.'

Yury explained his reasons for leaving the city and told Strelnikov about Tonya's connection to the Krueger family.

'None of that is important now, as you know, Comrade. I see you were a medical doctor in the army. Why aren't you helping us now?' asked Strelnikov.

'I have my papers. I left the army after I was wounded twice.'

'Well, these are unusual times, dear doctor. Now you are free, as I said, but I have a feeling that we'll meet again. You may have a greater purpose in our plan than being a farmer in Varykino. For now, take care,' said Strelnikov as he sent Yury away.

When he was alone, the Army Commissar looked out of the window towards Yuryatin where he and his wife and daughter had lived. Were they still there? Couldn't he go to them? But they belonged to another life. First he had to finish his work for the revolution. Then, one day he could go back. But when? When would he see Lara and Katya again?

◆

The train left the station soon after Yury was sent back by Strelnikov, and two stops later, the Zhivagos finally got off. They were the only passengers to leave the train at Varykino, and after the train had disappeared, Tonya could hear the birds and smell the countryside. 'How lovely!' she cried out. She could not say any more. She burst into tears.

There was an old man at the station with a carriage, and he offered to drive the Zhivagos to the Krueger estate. He had worked for Tonya's grandfather and recognised her immediately, but he warned her not to talk to other people about the Kruegers. That connection would not make her popular now that the bolsheviks had taken over.

Everyone in the little group, including Sasha, enjoyed the trip to the estate, but they were faced with an embarrassing situation when they arrived. Avercius Mikulitsin and his wife were living in the house that had been the estate manager's in the old days. Mikulitsin was an old-style revolutionary and supported the ideas of the bolsheviks but not all of their methods. His only son, Liberius, on the other hand, was a very important bolshevik leader, although he was not much more than twenty years old. Mikulitsin had worked for the Kruegers for more than twenty-five years, right up until the day when the land and factories were taken over by the government. Mikulitsin had taken advantage of the fine house and some of the gardens. Living there was not legal, but the local bolshevik officials had not noticed what was going on. Mikulitsin and his wife made it quite clear, though, that they were not interested in sharing their good luck with the Zhivagos, or in putting themselves in danger to help them.

But Mikulitsin was much kinder than he appeared at first. After a quiet evening of conversation with the Zhivagos, he had agreed to give them two rooms connected to the back of the big house to live in. Through the spring and summer he gave them farm equipment, seeds, animals and lots of advice. Both Mikulitsin and the Zhivagos were happy with the unspoken contract that they had worked out.

Chapter 10   1919

At the end of the summer of 1919, Yury finally had a bit of free time and began to write a diary. In it he wrote that he had found the strongest drug of all: good health and real need. Yury, Tonya and Gromeko worked very hard all day and then sat in their small sitting-room and read, sewed or repaired things every evening. As a family, they were closer than ever and very content. In fact, Yury wrote in his diary that his professional eye told him that Tonya was expecting another baby, although she wouldn't admit it yet.

Yury recorded his dreams and fears in his diary. Besides recognising the signs of Tonya's condition, he also saw the first signs of heart disease in himself. He kept his condition secret, but he knew that he would have the same problem that his mother had had. Sometimes he got very bad headaches and imagined that he heard a calm, beautiful voice. He knew that it was not Tonya or his mother speaking, but he wondered who it was.

Yury's great ambition was to write an important book about art or science – something new but useful as well. Tonya encouraged him to make regular trips to the library in Yuryatin and to return to his habit of studying and writing. Yury began going to the library two or three times a week and started to feel like he was part of Yuryatin.

One morning Yury was sitting in his usual seat in the library's reading room. He had a large pile of books on the table in front of him and was surrounded by other regular library users. He was ready for several hours of hard work.

He was concentrating on his books when he noticed a change in the room. At the far end there was a new reader. Yury immediately recognised Nurse Antipova. She was sitting with her back to him, speaking in a low voice to one of the women who worked in the reading room. This woman had looked ill all morning, but after whispering to Lara for a few minutes, she walked back to her desk smiling and looking very much improved. Several people noticed the change in the ill woman and looked up and smiled at Lara, but she was already lost in the book she was reading.

Yury wanted to go and speak to Lara, but he felt shy and did not want to interrupt her work. He turned away from her and tried to read his own books, but he kept thinking of Lara. Suddenly he knew that the calm, beautiful voice that came to him in his dreams was hers.

'She does not try to please people or to look beautiful, but that makes her lovelier than ever,' he thought. 'How well she does everything! She reads as if it was the simplest thing in the world, a thing that even animals could do.' He looked at her and felt completely peaceful. Then he went back to his studies with a smile on his lips.

After reading for several hours, Yury decided to speak to Lara, but when he looked up he found that she had left the library. He returned his books to the desk and accidentally saw a form with Lara's name and address on it. It wasn't many days before Yury went looking for her house.

The house was not difficult to find. Yury opened the gate and saw Lara fetching water. She looked amazed but remained natural in her manner. All she said was: 'Zhivago!'

'Larissa Fyodorovna!' whispered Yury.

'What are you doing here? Have you come to see me?' Lara asked.

'Who else?'

'Why didn't you speak to me in the library? I know you saw me.'

They walked into Lara's small flat like two old friends. They drank tea, talked about their children and discussed the revolution. Yury told Lara about meeting Strelnikov.

'You saw him!' Lara said in amazement. 'How extraordinary! What kind of impression did he make on you?'

'On the whole, very good. I think he is a brilliant man, one of a kind. He will be very important for the country, but, for some reason, I think he will fail in the end.'

'I must be honest with you before you say anything else. The Strelnikov you met is my husband, Pasha Antipov.'

'He can't be,' cried Yury. 'What do you have in common with such a man?'

'I don't understand everything he is doing, but I know that he believes in his goals. Maybe you think he doesn't love Katya and me, that he has forgotten us? Well, you are wrong. Someday he will be finished with fighting. Then he will come home to us and lay his victories at my feet.'

Just then Katya came in from school. Lara surprised the eight-year-old by lifting her up and holding her tightly.

◆

Two months later Yury was riding home from Yuryatin. For those two months he had been deceiving Tonya, lying to her about why he needed to stay some nights every week in Yuryatin. He had never chosen between Tonya and Lara. He still loved his wife and did not want to hurt her in any way. At home he felt like a criminal. He knew he was putting his family's happiness and safety at risk.

But now things would change. He had decided to tell Tonya everything and beg her to forgive him. He had told Lara that afternoon that he could not continue to be unfaithful to Tonya. Lara had listened calmly and agreed with Yury as tears rolled down her cheeks.

Yury was thinking about Lara and desperately wanted to see her again. He hadn't said anything to Tonya yet, so why couldn't he see Lara just one more time? He would make sure that she understood how much he truly loved her, and he would again explain, more gently this time, why he had to stop seeing her.

The thought of seeing Lara again made Yury's heart leap with happiness. He was picturing his next visit to her house when he heard a gun fired very close to him. Three men on horses stood in his path.

'Don't move, Comrade Doctor,' said the oldest of the three. 'If you obey orders, you will be perfectly safe. If you don't, it's very simple: we'll shoot you. Our army needs a doctor, and you've been chosen.'

'Are you Mikulitsin's son, Liberius?' asked Yury.

'No, but Comrade Liberius Forester is our leader. Now, follow us, and no funny business.'

Chapter 11   1919–21

Yury had been kidnapped by a group called the Forest Brotherhood. Such groups were considered by many people to be the true spirit of the Red Army during the Civil War. They were known for being untraditional, even a bit wild. The men who joined them came from all levels of society. There were peasants, soldiers from the German army, churchmen, students, disappointed politicians and true revolutionaries who were determined to see a new Russia.

One of the leaders of this enormous people's army was Comrade Liberius Forester, once known as Liberius Avercievich, the son of Avercius Mikulitsin from Varykino. He was the head of the Forest Brotherhood, and Dr Zhivago became their medical man for almost two years.

The young Liberius was respected by the leaders of the Red Army because he got results, and the Forest Brotherhood helped to drive the Whites, led by Kolchak, towards the east.

*The Forest Brotherhood were known for being untraditional,
even a bit wild.*

During Yury's time with them, the Brotherhood grew to ten
times its original size and made Liberius more famous than ever.

Unfortunately for Yury, he became one of Liberius's
favourites. He would invite Yury to his tent and keep him awake
with long, drunken explanations of his plans and ambitions. Yury
was opposed to Liberius in every way. First, he could not accept
the extreme acts of cruelty that he had witnessed by both sides in
the war. Second, he could not agree with the ideas that people
like Liberius wished to force on all Russians. And, finally, he
hated Liberius for kidnapping him and keeping him away from
his family. But Liberius was too interested in himself to notice
what Yury thought of him.

In the autumn of 1921, towards the end of the Civil War, Yury
was with the Brotherhood as they began to build their winter

camp. He was losing all patience with Liberius and was almost sick with worry about his family.

'Tonya, my darling, my poor child,' he prayed. 'Did you have our baby? Have we got a new little son or daughter? My dear ones, what is happening to you? Lara, I dare not speak your name or I will die. O God! O God! Please protect my loved ones. Please return me to them.'

Yury had lived all of his time with the Brotherhood with no news of his family or of Lara. He had heard rumours that the Whites had destroyed Yuryatin, but Liberius's information about even his own family could not be trusted.

That winter, the Brotherhood were safe inside their camp, deep in a large Siberian forest. They were surrounded by their enemies, but the Whites were too weak to cause any damage to them. The Whites made one last attempt to trick Liberius's men. They began to attack one corner of the camp. As a result, Liberius sent soldiers to that area to drive the Whites away. There they found a dying man with only one arm and one leg. His other arm and leg had been cut off and tied to his back. He was hardly able to crawl along on the ground. He spoke a few words with great difficulty: 'Look out, comrades. I am a warning.'

'Don't worry,' the soldiers told him. 'There are plenty of us in the camp.'

'The Whites want to surprise you. They want to boil you alive. They'll cut your children into pieces. They will make your wives their slaves. They'll . . .'

The poor man was unable to go on. He cried out without finishing his story. The soldiers took off their caps and made the sign of the cross. They knew this horrible and desperate act by the Whites to frighten them signalled the end of their enemies' power.

That night Yury was called to Liberius's tent for another 'conversation'. He pressed Liberius for news of Varykino but only got Liberius's aimless political ideas. Yury lost patience and stood up.

'Why are you putting on your coat? Where are you going?'

'I'll be back in a minute,' said Yury. 'There's a lot of smoke in here, and I've got a headache. I'll just go out for some air.'

Yury looked at the clear sky and imagined Tonya walking through a snow storm, carrying Sasha and a small baby. She dragged them through the snow with all her strength, but she couldn't keep going. She fell and the snow covered her and the children. There was no one to help them.

Suddenly Yury made a decision. He walked out of the camp without looking back. He passed the guards with no difficulty because he had learned the Brotherhood's secret words, and he kept going until he found the food, heavy clothes and boots that he had hidden under a big tree near the edge of the camp. He looked at the tree which was covered in snow, but he was no longer thinking of Tonya. The white branches reminded him of Lara's white arms, held out to him, ready to welcome him.

'I'll find you, my love, my heart, my life.'

It was a clear night with a full moon. Yury picked up his things and walked further into the forest.

♦

There was always a small crowd of people on the main square of Yuryatin. They stood silently, reading the latest announcements from the local government – lately taken over by the Reds – about work papers, housing, food allowances. It was no joke in those days not to know about any new rules; it might cost you your life.

Among the group of people trying to understand the most recent announcements on this fine spring day was a thin, wild-looking man with long hair and beard, wearing dirty bits of rags and old army boots. The people around him wondered if he was ill or insane, but they were used to seeing these forgotten men and didn't pay much attention to him. They would have been surprised to know that he was the brilliant doctor from Moscow: Yury Andreyevich Zhivago.

Yury had left Liberius's camp and walked from Siberia. He had followed the railway lines, most of which were out of action. He was witness to events that proved that the laws of human society had been forgotten. But now the sight of Yuryatin filled him with happiness, like the sight of a long-lost friend. He read as many of the announcements as he could and then walked slowly to Lara's house, not knowing if she still lived there or not.

No one was at home except for the rats who looked at Yury boldly before running off to their holes. Yury's heart jumped when he moved a brick and found the key where Lara always used to hide it. But imagine his surprise at finding a note there for him. He read it quickly:

What happiness! They say you are alive and have come back. Don't go anywhere. Wait for me in the flat. I've left some food for you – mostly potatoes – put the lid on the pot to keep the rats out.

You know that your family are in Moscow. Tonya has had a little girl. We'll talk about everything when we meet. You're alive – I'm mad with happiness!

Yury sat at the table and wept. He thought about Tonya and his children – now two of them. 'I can't think straight. How did my family get to Moscow? Are they all right? What will become of my darlings? I'll find them, even if I have to walk all the way to Moscow. I'll see them again, we'll be together one day.'

Yury's thoughts were going round in circles. He forced himself to eat some potatoes, and then he fell across Lara's bed. He woke up sweating and in tears. 'I've got a temperature, I'm ill,' he thought. 'Exhaustion, or perhaps typhus again. I must wait to see which is going to win, life or death. But I'm too sleepy to think.'

In the darkness, Yury wept and complained to himself. Each time he sat up a little, he realised that he could not move and fell back into a deep sleep again. Once he looked towards the window and thought, 'How long have I been lying here? Is it winter now?'

Then one day Yury realised that he was in a clean bed, wearing a clean shirt. He was comfortable and not hungry, thirsty or tired. An angel was sitting beside his bed, holding his hand. He had recovered because his angel, Lara, had washed him, fed him, been his doctor and nurse. Her care, her beauty, her whispered conversation had saved him.

It was easy and right for them to be together – and to be separated from the rest of the world. They were both disappointed at how the individual had been lost in the revolution. 'Do you remember what it was like when you were a child, Yury?' Lara asked one afternoon.

'I remember some things. What are you talking about?'

'I remember a long time when everything was peaceful. Even the future seemed full of peace. People listened to reason, and it was natural for everyone to act fairly in their business with each other. Murders and other violent actions only happened in the theatre, not in our daily lives.

'But then something false came into our country. Do you know what I think was the root of all the evil and blood and tears and insanity that we have gone through?'

'I'm not sure. Please go on,' said Yury.

'All of the evil happened when people stopped listening to the voices of individuals. It became old-fashioned to have personal beliefs. Everyone had to sing the same tune and follow the same leader. Everything was touched by this new "law": friendships, families, marriages, as well as politics. No one could act naturally, and so the individual was destroyed,' explained Lara.

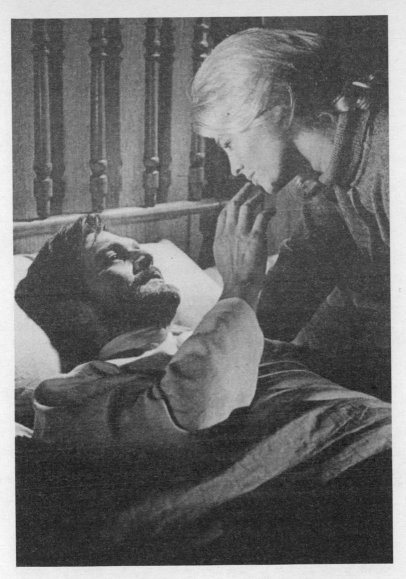

*An angel was sitting beside his bed. He had recovered
because his angel, Lara, had washed him, fed him,
been his doctor and nurse.*

Yury and Lara would talk about the revolution and its effects on society and the individual for hours; still, their great joy was their love. Most people experience love without noticing how remarkable it is, but Yury and Lara knew how lucky they were to have found each other.

Lara agreed that Yury should go to Moscow as soon as possible to find his family, but for now he was too weak. And so the happy couple, along with Lara's daughter, Katya, enjoyed a short time of peace and happiness in their own private world. Yury found a job at a hospital because they needed money and because it was dangerous to be unemployed, and Lara continued her day-to-day routine. But this situation could not last.

The new government was not kind to citizens who did not behave properly. The officials had their eyes on both Lara and Yury. It was thought that Yury's ideas were too independent. People began to talk about him at the hospital: he didn't follow the rules. He got all of his ideas from Nikolay Vedenyapin, his Uncle Kolya. He couldn't be trusted. He wasn't a good bolshevik.

Lara was in danger because the leaders knew that Strelnikov was Pavel Pavlovich Antipov, her husband. Pasha had never been a member of the Bolshevik Party, and after the Civil War he was no longer considered a hero. He had disappeared, and so it was logical for people to think he might get in touch with Lara and Katya.

'The air is getting thick,' said Lara one day. 'Our time of safety is over. They'll come after us soon, you and me. And then what will happen to Katya? I'm a mother. I must think of something – we must have a plan. These worries are driving me out of my mind.'

'I agree,' said Yury, 'but what can we do?'

'We can't escape,' answered Lara. 'There's nowhere to hide. But maybe we could get away from the officials' attention for a while.

Can we go to Varykino? No one goes there. Could we disappear there and live away from the dangers that surround us?'

'I don't know what to say, my darling. I must think about Moscow. Haven't you been telling me to go there? Why can't the three of us leave here and go to Moscow?'

'To Moscow? Yury, I can't. No, I have to stay. I must wait for Pasha and be here if he needs me.' For the moment, they were unable to make any decisions about their future.

A few days later in the evening, Yury and Lara were sitting at the table, discussing how to protect Katya. Someone rang the door bell and Lara walked quickly through the hall to open the door. Yury heard her talking to Glaphira, who worked at the central post office.

'I've brought a letter for your friend. It's lucky for him that I work at the post office. I don't know how many hands it's been through. It's from Moscow and it was sent five months ago. No one had heard of this Dr Zhivago until they asked me.'

The long letter, written on many pages, torn and dirty, was from Tonya. Yury found it in his hands without knowing how it had got there. He began to read it and forgot about his surroundings.

My darling Yury,

Do you know that we have a daughter? We have named her Masha in memory of your mother.

Now, more important news: several important people, professors, writers and others, including Uncle Kolya, my father and the rest of us must leave Russia. We are being sent away. This is a terrible thing because we don't know where you are or if you are all right, but it could have been much worse. If you were here, you could go with us. But where are you?

I am sending this letter to Antipova's address; I am sure that she will give it to you if she finds you. I am worried because I do not know how you will find us or if you will want to come to us one day. My heart tells me that you are still alive and I trust it. Maybe when you are found, things in our country will be calmer and we will not have any difficulty in being together again. But as I write this, I myself don't believe in the possibility of such happiness.

My greatest problem is that I love you and know that you don't love me. I keep trying to understand the reason for this. I look into myself and think about our life together. I cannot imagine how or when things started to go wrong. As for me, I love you and always will. I know of no one better than you in the world.

Nothing has been decided finally, but it looks like we will go to Paris, where you lived as a small boy. Father is well and both of the children. Sasha is a big, strong boy and he misses you very much.

You know that I met your Lara. She was very kind to me at Varykino, but I can see that she is the opposite of me. I was born to make life simple and to look for solutions. She was born for a complicated life, with adventure.

God keep you. I must stop because a man has come for this letter. My darling husband, my children's father, what has happened to us? Do you realise that we'll never, never see each other again?

When he received Tonya's letter, Yury lost his reason for going to Moscow. His family were beyond his reach, but at least now he knew that they were out of Russia and safe. He got up the next day and continued to work at the hospital, not knowing what might happen to him and Lara.

One winter evening, Yury walked through the heavy snow after work. When he arrived at the flat, Lara met him in the hall. 'Komarovsky is here,' she said. She looked very frightened, as if someone had struck her.

'What? Why has he come here?' demanded Yury.

'He says he is going to the Far East. He has been given a very high position in the new government in that part of the country. He will be the Minister of Justice. He says that we are in great danger – you and I and Pasha – and that he can save us, if we follow his advice.'

'I'm going out. I will not see him,' said Yury as he turned to go outside again.

Lara threw herself at Yury's feet and grabbed his legs. 'Please, talk to him, Yury. He's practical and experienced. I realise you find him disgusting, but please, for my sake, put your feelings to one side and listen to him. Just for a few minutes.'

Yury could not deny Lara's request. He followed her into the sitting-room and looked at Komarovsky with a hatred that he could not hide. This was the man who had stolen Lara's childhood. He had made her discover life too early and forced her to experience things that she was not prepared for. Lara believed that Komarovsky had not only spoilt her early years, but that the effects of knowing him had also damaged her marriage to Pasha.

Komarovsky was also the man who Yury considered to be responsible for his father's death. Yury believed that he was an orphan because of this man who Lara was asking him to rely on for advice and help.

He walked into the room and Komarovsky spoke to him in a familiar manner. 'My dear young man. As you know, I was a great friend of your father's. He died in my arms. He was a wonderful, generous man. But I see you look more like your mother. She was a gentle dreamer, and a great beauty.'

'Excuse me, sir,' Yury interrupted, 'Lara has asked me to see you. She said that you had some business with me. I agreed, but haven't chosen to meet you, and I don't consider you as a friend. Do not speak about my father and mother. What is it that you want?'

'Calm down, young Zhivago. There's no reason to lose your temper. I'll come straight to the point: I've been here in Yuryatin for two days, and in that short time I've learnt many things about the two of you – more than you know about yourselves. Neither of you measure up to the new bolshevik style. The officials will not be tolerant for much longer. You cannot afford to pretend that you are safe, and that no one is watching you. The police will come for you any day now.

'You, Dr Zhivago, are a man,' continued Komarovsky. 'You are your own master and can act foolishly if you choose to, but Lara Fyodorovna is not so free. She is a mother, and she is gambling with her child's life. She must play by the official rules to protect her daughter.'

'And you think that you are the man who can save us?' asked Yury with a sound of disgust in his voice.

'Yes, I can and I will if you will use your head and accept my offer. Because of my new position, I can take the three of you with me to Vladivostok. From there you can easily get a boat and join your family in Paris. I have also promised Lara that I will save Strelnikov if possible. My men can look for him in Eastern Siberia and help him to escape into the region where I will be in control.'

When Lara heard the plan for her and Katya – and for Yury and Pasha – she said to Yury: 'You see, darling, how important all of this is for us and for Pasha.'

'Lara, why should we trust this man? For my part,' Yury said, looking at Komarovsky, 'I do not intend to let you control my life in any way. As for Lara and Strelnikov, that is Lara's decision.'

'You know, without my saying anything,' said Lara to Yury, 'that I would not go without you.'

The three argued for several hours, but in the end, they all refused to change from their original positions. Komarovsky kept talking about the political importance of Mongolia, and the possibility of a new life there for Yury and Lara, but they had stopped listening. They wanted him to leave so that they could talk to each other. Finally, they showed him to the door.

After Komarovsky's visit, Lara and Yury began to notice more signs which proved that the older man was right: their situation was growing more dangerous. Every evening they talked about what steps they should take. Finally, Yury said, 'Why don't we go to Varykino, as you suggested in the first place? At least we might have a few weeks of peace.'

'Oh, Yury! How glad I am! Can we go quickly, without delay? It will be wonderful to be away from our problems.'

'Are you sure you want to go, Lara?' asked Yury. 'Komarovsky is still in Yuryatin, and your position is different from mine. You do not need to share my danger. You can go with him and protect Katya.'

'Yury, my darling, you are my strength and my happiness. I want to be with you and nowhere else. Let's go to Varykino and forget about the world of politics. When we get there, I will tell you some good news.'

'I feel exactly the same,' said Yury. He didn't say anything about Lara's news because he thought he already knew that she would tell him she was expecting a baby. 'I think that death is knocking at our door, so why don't we live our final days as we choose. Let us be alone together for the last time before we are separated. We'll speak to each other in our own secret language, we'll live in our own world, and we'll be surrounded by our love.'

They left town on the morning of a grey winter's day, without telling anyone where they were going. The three of them laughed and sang as the horse and carriage raced along the road to Varykino.

When they arrived, they decided against living in the house that Yury had lived in with his family. It held too many painful memories for him. Instead, they moved into the bigger house that had been Mikulitsin's. Yury walked into the large, elegant office and immediately made plans to begin writing again. Then all three of them lay down without undressing, using their coats as blankets. They fell into a deep, enjoyable sleep, like children who had been running and playing all day in the open air.

The next morning they began a routine which satisfied all three of them so long as they didn't think about the outside world. Katya found Liberius's old books and playthings and was happy in the peace and comfort of the big house. Lara enjoyed

They left town on the morning of a grey winter's day,
without telling anyone where they were going.

her role of wife and mother and thought about a new baby. She cleaned rooms, washed clothes and cooked for her little family. Yury took care of the horse, found wood for fuel, carried water and helped Lara all day. Then in the evenings, he went to the office and wrote far into the night. He re-wrote old poems, began new ones and made plans for many other kinds of books. Yury's heart was at peace, and he experienced the feeling that his writing was controlled by something which was outside him and above him. His writing and Lara's nearness made him feel whole.

But there was no way that Yury and Lara could avoid the wider world. Every night, a group of wolves came to the house, and each night they got bolder and came closer until Yury went outside and frightened them away. Lara thought that the wolves were a bad sign, and she began to worry about their safety again. She wanted Yury to find a better place for them to hide, but they had run out of hiding places.

One morning Yury returned to the house with his arms full of wood and found Komarovsky there, talking to Lara. 'Yury!' she cried. 'Where have you been? We need you here.'

'I have been to fetch more wood. Why is everyone standing? Sir, please sit down,' said Yury politely.

'Yury, aren't you amazed to see Victor Ippolitovich? Victor, tell him. Tell him quickly.' Lara was very nervous.

'Yes, you're right, Lara. This must be done quickly. I have allowed the rumour that I have left Yuryatin to be heard around the town. People think that I have already left for Vladivostok, but I have come to get you, to take the three of you with me. My official train is waiting for us, but we must go now, there is not one minute to lose.'

'I don't understand you, Komarovsky. You talk as if I have agreed to come with you. Go and good luck to you, and let Lara go with you if she wishes, but I will not go with you,' said Yury calmly.

'What is this <u>nonsense?</u>' shouted Lara. '"If Lara wishes!" You know that I will not go without you.'

'So you have decided?' said Komarovsky. 'But, please, with Lara's permission, may I speak to you, Dr Zhivago, alone for two minutes?'

'Certainly. If it's so important, we can go into the kitchen,' said Yury.

They left Lara in the sitting-room, full of worry. 'Strelnikov has been <u>captured</u> and shot,' Komarovsky reported to Yury.

'How awful! Are you really sure?' asked Yury.

'It's what I have been told, and I'm quite certain that it's true.'

'Don't tell Lara,' warned Yury. 'She'll go out of her mind if she finds out.'

'That's why I'm talking to you. You must make her leave here. Don't you see? The police will be looking for her now more than ever. You must tell her to leave with me. Pretend that you will catch up with us as quickly as possible. Lie to her if necessary, but make her come with me,' said Komarovsky.

'I'll <u>obey</u> you for Lara's sake. I know that we'll be separated soon one way or another. I'll talk to her.'

'You should come, too, you know.'

'Yes, I know, but I don't want to owe my life to you. One day I may come to you and beg you to save me, but not now. For now, I'll worry about Lara. I'll worry about myself tomorrow,' said Yury sadly.

Yury watched Lara and Katya leave with Komarovsky. He stood at the big window in the office and wept; his heart was breaking. 'What have I done?' he asked himself. 'I have sent away my reason for living. And she doesn't know that I have tricked her. She thinks that I'll join her in Yuryatin before the train leaves. We didn't even say goodbye properly. I didn't even kiss her.'

Yury watched the carriage disappear and then they were gone.

Still standing at the window, he thought, 'My bright sun has gone down. My life has finished.'

Over the next few days, something was going on with Yury that made no sense. He stopped taking care of the house, or the horse, or himself. He lost count of the days and forgot to eat or sleep. He drank vodka and wrote poems for Lara. When he did sleep, he had frightening dreams about her. She was standing before him, holding out her arms to him, but he could not reach her.

A few days later, Yury heard someone approaching the house on foot. How odd. He was sure that Komarovsky or the police would come on horses. Who could it be? His visitor opened the door and confidently walked in. He obviously knew his way around the house.

Yury was sitting in the office, listening to the footsteps get nearer. The stranger opened the door of the office and looked directly at Yury. He was a powerful, handsome man. 'Strelnikov,' whispered Yury in amazement.

Strelnikov started talking almost immediately and did not want to stop. It was as if he had made an important decision and did not want to be alone with it. He and Yury shared their ideas about what they called the revolutionary madness of the times, and Pasha was determined to look into every corner of his own life. He wanted to be judged and would not stop talking until he had told Yury everything that he felt guilty about from the last ten years.

Then they talked about Lara. 'You can't imagine how lovely she was as a child, as a schoolgirl. You have no idea,' said Pasha.

'Oh, but I did see her once in those days,' said Yury. I saw her on the night that her mother tried to kill herself. I still remember how she looked.'

'Yes, well, I did everything for the sake of that girl. I studied, became a teacher and left Moscow for Yuryatin. I kept studying for her <u>sake</u>, and then went off to war to show her that I was good and brave. After I escaped from the Germans, I had to finish my life's work before I could return to her. But now I would give anything for one look at her and my daughter. When she used to come into a room it was as if the window flew open and the room filled with air and light.'

'I know how much you loved her. But forgive me, have you any idea of her love for you? She loved you more than anyone or anything in the world,' said Yury.

'What makes you say that?'

'She told me,' said Yury. 'She said that you were the example of what a human being should be, a man who had no equal. She said that your sincerity was beyond question and that if she could go back to the home she had shared with you, she would crawl on her hands and knees from the ends of the earth.'

When the two men finally stopped talking, Yury put Pasha in the next room, and then he went to bed and had the first good night's sleep that he had had since Lara left. He woke up with a headache because he had slept too long. At first he couldn't think where he was.

Then he remembered: 'Strelnikov is in there. He must be up by now. I'll go to the kitchen and make us some coffee.'

He knocked on the door of Pasha's room but got no answer. He wasn't in the room and Yury couldn't find him anywhere in the house. 'He's probably gone out for a walk,' he thought.

Yury lit the fire, picked up a bucket and went outside for water. A few yards from the door, Pasha lay across the path. He had shot himself and the snow around his head looked like a soft red pillow.

Strelnikov was dead and Lara was gone. Yury left the house and began his final journey – to Moscow.

62

Chapter 12   Spring, 1922

After a long, frightening struggle to get home, Yury walked into the great city, thinner and more worn out than when he had arrived in Yuryatin after escaping from the Forest Brotherhood. He had sold most of his clothes and wore a few old rags to cover his thin, broken body. He was not noticed among the thousands of Red Army men who crowded the stations and the streets of the city.

He did not arrive alone. He had travelled across the country with the young peasant boy, Vassya, whom he had met again on his journey. After all of their experiences, they were both extremely shy and stood quietly in the street or in rooms where Yury was still welcomed. In such rooms Yury heard the story of his family's departure from Moscow.

This odd couple found a way of living that suited both of them and allowed them to stay away from the noise and crowds of the city. Vassya had some talent as an artist, and so Yury, with help from a few old friends, found him a place at the Stroganov Institute. Eventually the boy specialised in designing and printing books.

After a while, Yury began writing short books on a variety of subjects and Vassya put them together. These books contained Yury's philosophy of life, his views on medicine, his definitions of health and sickness, his thoughts on history and religion, as well as poems, short stories and descriptions of places he had seen throughout his life. The books were written in a conversational style, and they became very popular, although Yury's opinions were considered progressive, and sometimes dangerous.

Eventually the friendship between Yury and Vassya cooled. The boy was eager to make something of his life, and he looked for ways to work within the new system. Yury, on the other hand, wanted to close himself off from the world and forget about people and politics. The boy left, and Yury gave up medicine completely, stopped seeing friends and lived alone with his thoughts.

City life was not like it had been twenty years earlier. It was difficult to get food and impossible to have enough heat, light or water. The citizens of Moscow were unhealthy and unwashed most of the time. But one family was doing better than most, and they were able to help Yury. This was the family of Markel who had been the chief servant at the grand home of Alexander Alexandrovich Gromeko – Tonya's home – and the house in which Yury had grown up.

Markel was in charge of a large apartment building, and he and his family lived in the rooms under the ground floor. Unlike the rest of the building, these rooms were always dry and warm because of an enormous oven, and they had an endless amount of hot water. Markel and his family felt rich, indeed. They helped Yury because he was totally alone and because he had become strange and quite helpless.

Dr Zhivago, as the family knew him, was in and out of the Markels' flat every day to get water. And before the parents noticed, their elder daughter had begun to help Yury in little ways. She sewed his clothes, cleaned his room and took food to him. And, before much longer, she was staying in Yury's room, and Markel was talking about 'my daughter, the doctor's wife'.

Chapter 13   Summer, 1929

Yury and his third 'wife', Marina, now lived with their two children in a flat near Misha Gordon's house. Yury still avoided a normal life and relied on Marina to look after the house and children. She worked at the post office and kept the family together.

Yury often spent Sunday afternoons in Misha's house, talking about the past and about the politics of the day. Yury would get bored with Misha and his friends but listened to them politely because he loved Misha so much.

One day, Misha made Yury sit down and listen to him with both ears. Misha had a list of things that he wanted his old friend to do: first, contact Tonya in Paris so that he could make Marina his legal wife; second, pay attention to what was happening in the country and learn to follow the rules; and, finally, go back to work. Misha believed that Yury was too talented to waste his life.

'You must wake up and make something of your life.'

'You're right, Misha. I've been thinking about my life recently, too; I promise you that I am going to change. And quite soon, too. Honestly – you'll see. I'm not yet forty years old. I want to live and to do something important.

'But now, I can't stay any longer,' said Yury. 'Thank you for worrying about me, but I must go. I'm having difficulty breathing – it's the smoke and too many people. I'll go now or I'll have an attack. Thank you, Misha, you're a good friend. Goodbye.'

Next morning Marina came running to Misha's house. She was very upset because Yury had not come home the night before. She had the baby in one arm and was dragging the other child along. No one knew where Yury was so they searched for him for three days and nights.

◆

Yury had left Misha Gordon's house determined to make a new start. By chance, he ran into his half-brother, Yevgraf, and the two of them planned Yury's future. Yevgraf, as always, knew how to make things happen. He found Yury a small flat, made him eat properly, encouraged him to write and got him a job in the Botkin Hospital.

After the first three days with Yevgraf, Yury wrote to Marina. He told her that he had left in order to re-build his life. He did not want her or their children to be ashamed of him. He would return to them as soon as he had a job and was in control of his future. Unfortunately, Yury was not given enough time to see his future come to life.

One morning at the end of August Yury took the train to his new job. The train stopped and started over and over again and the crowded carriage became hotter and hotter. Yury felt desperate for air and tried to open the nearest window, but as he pulled on the window, he felt an unfamiliar pain. He knew that something had torn in his heart. The next time the train stopped, Yury fought his way through the crowd and got off. He took three steps and fell to the pavement. He never got up.

◆

Yury's coffin was visited by a stream of people who had known him at different times in his life. Many came because they had read his books and poems, others because they had known him as a brilliant doctor, and a few came because they were his true friends.

One woman walked into the room where the coffin lay, and, without a word, everyone else left her alone with the dead man. Now only Lara and Yury were in the room. She fought back her tears as long as she could, but then they burst from her, pouring down her cheeks and falling on her dress, her hands and the coffin.

'Oh, what a love it was, so free, so new, like nothing else on earth! A love that writers can imagine, but most people never know.'

◆

Lara stayed for several days with Yevgraf in Moscow. She helped him to organise Yury's papers, and he helped her to search for a child. This was the reason that she had been in Moscow at the time of Yury's death. She was looking for an eight-year-old girl who had been raised by strangers. There were many of these lost children in Moscow, but Lara did not find the one she was searching for.

One day Lara left Yevgraf's house and did not come back. She must have been picked up in the street by the police, still a common practice in those days. She disappeared or died, forgotten as a nameless number in one of the many women's prisons in the north.

Chapter 14   Summer, 1943

Misha Gordon was an officer in the Soviet army during World War II. He spent a lot of time with another officer, Major Dudorov, who had also been a good friend of Yury's when the three of them had been at school in Moscow. Both of these men had been political prisoners more than once in the time between the First and Second World Wars.

'I hear Zhivago — the general, Yury's brother, is in this area,' said Misha.

'Really? Why is that?' asked Dudorov.

'He thinks he has found his niece, the child of Yury and Larissa Fyodorovna Antipova. He has been looking for her since 1929 when Yury died and Lara disappeared.'

'But where did he find her?'

'She's here,' said Misha. 'She's the girl who does the laundry for our camp. I'm sure you know her. She smiles like Yury and has the same nose and eyes.'

'You mean Tanya Out-of-turn?'

'Yes, that's what they call her. Poor girl. She remembers her mother a little, and a man called Komarov, but it must have been

67

Komarovsky. Anyway, Tanya knew that this man wasn't her father. He didn't want children around and so her mother asked a young couple to look after Tanya for a while. She meant to come back for her, but the child never saw her mother again. Eventually she ran away from the couple and became one of the homeless children who wandered through the country after the Civil War. She's had a very rough life and no education.'

'But Yevgraf will look after her now,' said Dudorov.

'Yes, that's true.' After a few minutes of silence Misha added: 'But this kind of thing has happened several times in the course of history. A thing that is born from a great love or from great ideas becomes rough and common. Rome came out of Greece and the Russian Revolution came out of the Russian enlightenment.'

◆

About ten years later, on a quiet summer evening, the two friends – Misha Gordon and Dudorov – were reading a book of Yury's writings as they looked down on Moscow. They felt a peaceful joy for this city, for the whole land and for their children and grandchildren. They had faith in a new freedom of spirit, and a silent happiness filled them. They looked forward to the future and believed that Yury's book would give them the strength that they would need.

ACTIVITIES

Chapters 1–5

Before you read

1 Look at the front cover and the pictures in this book.
  a What do the clothes worn by the people suggest to you?
  b Look at the first and last chapter headings. How many years does the story cover?

2 These words all come in this part of the story. Use your dictionary to check their meaning.
  carriage   client   cottin   elegant   estate
  gambling   peasant   revolutionary   suicide
  Match each word with one of the meanings below:
  a an agricultural worker without much education
  b a vehicle pulled by horses
  c spending money by making bets
  d the act of killing oneself
  e a customer
  f a big country house and the land belonging to it
  g the wooden box in which a dead person is buried
  h tasteful and fashionable
  i belonging to a time of sudden political change

After you read

3 Who are they? Give the *full* name of each person, where you can.
  a a young boy whose mother has just died
  b his uncle, who looks after him
  c his father's lawyer
  d the young boy's closest friend
  e a beautiful girl, whose mother has a dress shop
  f her best friend, living with neighbours

4 Answer these questions:
  a What emergency interrupts the Gromekos' musical evening?
  b In Amalia's house, who are the two people observed secretly by Yury and Misha?
  c a How does Lara escape from Komarovsky?

d What dramatic event takes place at the Sventitskys' Christmas party?

e What tragedy takes place that same evening?

Chapters 6–8

Before you read

5   Some of the young people in this list get married: Yury, Pasha, Tonya, Lara, Rodya, Nadya. Can you guess who marries whom? Discuss your ideas with other students.

6   These words appear in this part of the story. Use a dictionary to learn their meaning.

   reindeer   typhus

Put each word in one of the sentences below:

   a ..... is a dangerous disease, caused by bad living conditions.

   b ..... are animals that live in the far north.

After you read

7   Answer these questions:

   a What did Pasha decide to do after four years in Yuryatin?

   b How did Yury become a patient in an army hospital?

   c Who does he meet again there?

8   'They stayed in the house for three days and nights, waiting to see who would be in control.'

   What event made Yury and his family stay indoors? Who was fighting whom?

9   Answer these questions:

   a Who was the boy with the reindeer cap and coat?

   b How did he help Yury and his family?

Chapters 9–10

Before you read

10   Consider the difficulties of living in Moscow during the winter of 1917–18. Do you think that Yuri and his family were right to leave the city when they did? How might life be better for them at Varykino? Discuss these questions with other students.

11 Choose the right answer.

  a *Comrade* means:

    (i) friend and companion

    (ii) family member

    (iii) soldier

  b A *labour gang* means:

    (i) a group of criminals

    (ii) a team doing heavy physical work

    (iii) a political party for workers

After you read.

12 Answer these questions:

  a How does Yury get into trouble during the train journey?

  b Which famous person allows him to go free?

13 Put these events in the correct order:

  a Yury visits Lara at her home.

  b The Zhivagos are given rooms at Varykino.

  c Lara tells Yury that Strelnikov is her husband, Pasha.

  d Yury is taken away by Liberius Forester's men.

  e Yury decides to end his love affair with Lara.

  f Yury sees Lara in the library at Yuryatin.

Chapter 11

Before you read

14 What sudden changes have occurred in Yury's life so far? What was the reason for each of them? Discuss these things with other students?

15 These words come in this part of the story. Use a dictionary to learn their meaning.

  craw   rags   wolf

Match each word with the right definition below:

  a a wild animal like a dog, found in some northern countries

  b to move slowly, close to the ground, like an insect

  c torn pieces of clothing or cloth

16 Yury is against Liberius for three reasons. What are they?

17 Who says these words? Who to?

    a 'You know that I will not go without you.'

    b 'One day I may come to you and beg you to save me but not now.'

    c 'I kept studying for her sake and then went off to war to show her that I was good and brave.'

Chapters 12–14

Before you read

18 In this last part of the book do you think that Yury will be reunited with his wife and children or with Lara? Why do you think so?

19 'The Russian Revolution came out of the Russian *Enlightenment*.' (page 68) Check the meaning of this word in your dictionary. *Enlightenment* means:

    a the age of reason

    b the age of freedom

    c the age of electricity

After you read

20 What part do the following people play in the last years of Yury's life?

    a Vassya   **b** Marina   **c** Yevgraf

21 In the last part of the book, Tanya appears.

    a What is her job?

    b Who are her parents?

Writing

22 Yury was very upset by two events on the evening of the Sventitskys' Christmas party in 1911. Imagine that you are Yury. Write about that evening in your diary.

23 Imagine that you are Pasha. Just before you kill yourself, you write a short letter to Lara, expressing your love for her and explaining why you never returned home.

24 It is 1919. Lara is living in Yuryatin and Tonya at Varykino. Yury is with the Forest Brotherhood. The two women meet by accident. Write the conversation between them.

25 Yury lives with three different women and has a child or children with each of them. Do you blame him for this? Attack or defend his behaviour, according to your point of view.

26 It has been said that the form of this novel is shaped by the historical events it describes. Give examples from the story that support this idea.

27 Write a report on this book for other students in your class. Say what you liked and disliked about it, with reasons for your opinions.